≈YP≈

YOUR

Between poems,
several pages have been left blank.
I call them "your page." They are there for
your words –
notes, thoughts, poetic lines and verse.
I hope their empty spaces call to you.

CONTENTS

POEMS FOR MEN

BROTHER

Dear brother,
my blood and bone.

You blow your warm breath
on my frozen cheek.

You wink at my worn-out jokes,
poke fun at my overly serious side.

You touch my shoulder when I cry,
offer me your hand when I fall down.

You bear hug me when I get frenzied,
tell me with few words when I'm wrong.

You teach me to take a punch, push through
pain, practice patience, acceptance and tolerance.

You are Mom and Dad's best gift to me. Even
now, you are with me when I feel alone at night.

THE DUKE AND MY DAD

"Dad, you're staring."
It was 1978, in a Newark diner.
"That's the Duke!" Dad whispered.
"Who?"

"The booth behind you."
Subtly as I could, I turned.
Seated alone, John Wayne,
holding a mug of black coffee.

Dad was up before I could
say *noooo*. By the time I reacted,
he was shaking the Duke's hand;
both were laughing.

When Dad returned,
His face was different,
like he had seen a saint,
an authentic holy man.

Mr. Wayne stood up,
took out his wallet and left a tip,
paid at the register in cash,
turned to my father, winked, and left.

As he walked away,
I asked my father what he had said.
"He told me, 'Ride tall,
and leave a good tip.'"

Both John Wayne and my father
died the following year, but not
before giving me their way to see
the world, and a code to live by.

OUR DAY TOGETHER

We walk in the park
where we first met.

We sit on the porch
watching the world get wet.

We lie quietly in bed
feeling perfectly blessed.

I gently touch your face.
You put your paw on my chest.

DRUMBEAT

My drum set sat in our basement
next to my mother's washing machine.
She encouraged me to drum,
"Practice is what you need." I resisted,
"Practice is so boring." What I liked to do
was wait until she put a load of wash in,
wait for her to go back upstairs, and then I'd
wail away to the rhythm of the machine.

The washer had a mechanical sound
that repeated like a metronome and
the water crashing against the tub
sounded like ocean waves. Clink-clank,
squish, squash, clink-clank, squish squash.
Then after a short while, a thud
followed by a whirling sound that cued me
to do a drumroll on my cymbals.

When the wash and spin cycles were over,
and the machine was done, I'd go crazy
and hit every drum and cymbal I had until
I was exhausted by my crescendo. My mother
never told me to stop fooling around. Maybe
she didn't hear me down in the basement.
On the other hand, she could hear me
whisper a secret to my best friend.

PLATO THE SEAGULL

A yolk-colored sun scrambles
above a charcoal horizon
flat as a table-top, another
extraordinary shore day begins.
I'm hungry for more of what it offers:
salty air, silky sand and blinding light.
Can't get enough of this stuff, another
chance at heaven, another day in Eden.
I'm not greedy, I'm willing to share.
There's more than enough for all of us.
At the beach, a seagull can be generous,
and smugly philosophical.

There is nothing to writing poetry.
All you do is sit down with your notebook
and open a vein.

after Red Smith

≈YP≈

COWBOY

I never told you this:
when I was a kid,
I longed to be a cowboy,
a man with an iron code,

who honored women,
and respected the old,
a hero indifferent to
what others thought of him,

who stood tall and talked straight,
when he talked at all.

In Dallas, back in December,
I bought a handsome western
hat, leather band and all,
kept it on my closet top shelf.

Last night I showed it to you.
You laughed, big belly laughs.
Maybe I should have told you,
I always wanted to be a cowboy.

DERRICK – MY GERMAN FRIEND

Derrick died without warning,
there was no time for goodbye,
my Fatherland friend and colleague
with a sadness in his eye.

He was born at attention
during an outrageous war,
unthinkably, good Germans
did all they could to ignore.

Through parents and two sisters,
he was tailored not for arms,
schooled in language and culture,
gentlemanly, peaceful charms.

He hoped that in America,
he'd moved beyond his shame.
He told me of his secret,
that in bone, he still felt the blame.

Derrick is home in his harbor,
while we are still out to sea.
His was an inner struggle,
at last, he's finally free.

MISS WEGLE

German granite
chiseled into a five-foot cylinder.
Thick fingers that grasped
you in a handshake
full of strength and lift.
She was unquestionable discipline
always speaking in a calm voice.
In her sixth-grade classroom
the morning schedule was
as dependable as sunrise.
Only a Russian atomic attack
could compromise morning reading at 9.
In her mind reading was fundamental
years before others named it so.
I struggled with reading, but
my strength was arithmetic at 10.
For world geography at 11, each country
had its own page in our notebooks.
She liked a tiny drawing I did for Brazil -
wrote "Good" in red on my page.
I was elated.

We memorized lengthy passages,
Longfellow's "Ride of Paul Revere"
and Lincoln's "Gettysburg Address."
Somehow, she made it all achievable.
She understood how much
simple rewards, words or gold stars,
could mean to a nascent pupil.
At eleven years old,
I was less than a larva
thriving in her care, taking comfort
in her dependable routine
with its impregnable order.
I was her child for the year.
She was my gold star teacher
teaching me to fly.

WORKERS

Across
the street,
workers me-
thodically add
strip by strip of
grey shingle to my
neighbor's roof, from
bottom left to top right,
careful not to step off the
ever-present edge, or let
gravity take them down the
incline. No wandering mind
could survive this task. They work
silently without stopping as the sun
tests their resolve. Then one of them,

who had escaped the roof, returns, climbs
the ladder with a paper bag, reaches in and
with Tommy-John-precision, throws each of
them a can of coke. They sit on their work and
drink the cold rejuvenator. Their rest is brief,
less than a few minutes, their sweat dries,
and then it's back to their labor. They must
finish their work before sunset, so they can
go home to their wives, kids and dinner.
Then dream about clouds.

Tomorrow there will be another roof.

A poem can ambush you.

after Paul Carroll

DUST

I am only dust trying to be a man.
All I can do is the best I can.

I Am Only Dust trying to be a man.
Sometimes I fought, sometimes I ran.

I Am Only Dust Trying To Be A Man.
When I loved and lost, I loved again.

I AM ONLY DUST TRYING TO BE A MAN.
I asked for help and God gave me a hand.

I am only dust trying to be a man…

ALUMNI

Ernie, Marine volunteer
right out of high school,
pocked face, virile,
a bit scary back then,
died at 18 in Viet Nam.

Mary, sweet girl
with a soft gentle voice,
high school valedictorian,
scholarship winner,
died at 36, unmarried.

Jerry, attorney like his
mom and dad, married
his sweetheart, raised sons
and a sizeable practice, died
at 48 from an unkind cancer.

Braver and brighter,
bolder than I,
deserving more,
now gone, undone,
and I am still here.

THE FISHING LESSON

The first time my Dad took me fishing
we brought a brown bag full of worms.
He selected a big, fat one for his hook,
a small one for mine. I didn't mind.
He saw I was reluctant to pierce
the worm with my hook. Without a word,
he took them from me. I didn't mind.
I was anxious and pulled the line before
he was done. The hook caught his finger,
blood beaded up. I thought he'd be angry,
but he didn't yell at me. After an hour,
he suggested we leave. I didn't mind.
He hadn't caught any fish.
I only caught his finger.
He didn't mind.

≈YP≈

FATHER JOHN AND ME

John Joyce was not a priest.
He was an extraordinary soul, proud father
of his only child, a daughter, caretaker of his
invalid wife, my high school chemistry teacher,
a model of manhood for me.

He was there when I returned home,
four years after high school graduation,
my BS in hand, teaching in an adjacent
classroom, wanting to be like him.
He never stopped teaching me.

He was my mentor,
taught me by example,
how to treat students,
how to prepare lively lessons,
even the difficult ones.

He read The Kiplinger Weekly Newsletter,
an insightful, middle-of-the-road assessment
of what was going on in the world.
He kept up and shared what he learned.
Now I read it each week.

He retired at 60 to his home in the countryside,
chopped firewood all summer and fall,
baked cookies, proud of his secret ingredient,
ground black walnuts,
took care of his wife every day until his last.

He never raised his voice,
or criticized others.
He was more than a friend;
he was my teacher, and
I learned and learned and learned from him.

MY ROMAN HOLIDAY

The Riviera - was
more than I expected,
both men and women
swam unprotected

from an undressed sun
that was ablazing,
their nonchalance
was most amazing.

My Puritan ways
were evaporating
as I studied their
foreplay for mating.

Off came my glasses,
my bathing suit too,
for when in Rome,
do as the Romans do.

AN EDUCATED MAN

Miss Wegle,
my learned teacher,
told us the story
of an average man
marooned on an island
with only two books –
the Bible and a dictionary.
He used his time advantageously
systematically studying them
and when sailors rescued him,
they found him to be
an educated man with
a sense of both justice
and compassion. I knew
Miss Wegle was such a man.

PACIFIC ISLANDS
– ALL IN A ROW –
A MARINE TRIBUTE

Overloaded landing crafts, all in a row,
standing room only
for lionhearted Marines
not thinking of tomorrow.

Marine warriors, all in a row,
assaulting the beach,
taking it before dark,
or die trying.

Marine tents, all in a row,
days of discipline and routine.
Morning sick call, treating all,
all except broken hearts.

Marines standing, all in a row,
Sunday services,
so many faiths, only one prayer.
Get us home.

Six Marines, all in a row,
raising the American flag
over an Pacific island
called Iwo Jima.

Six thousand Marine graves, all in a row,
crosses standing,
silently declaring,
I am here. Never give up.

Semper Fi

The child is father of the man.

William Wordsworth

BLOOD BROTHERS

When Cain killed Abel
he became a label
warning with this fable
a lesson for all time.

He tried lying
tearfully crying
even denying
this was his crime.

Farmer vs. herder
jealousy's murder
nothing's absurder
turning blood to brine.

Although so vain
Abel still loved Cain
brothers just the same
blood brothers of mine.

SENIOR DELUSION

There's no fool like an old fool
I heard you say to me,
but I'd be a fool if I didn't try,
even at seventy-three.

She's young and cute and very sharp.
You know she laughed at my joke.
Given a chance, if I get her number,
I'll invite her for fries and a coke.

You might say I'm overweight,
and haven't run a mile in years,
but you don't know what I have in mind,
doesn't involve climbing stairs.

First, she'll need some imagination
to raise her expectations a bit,
so when I kiss her in the dark,
she'll think she's kissing Brad Pitt.

HALF

An Israeli half-brother, I didn't know I had,
showed up at my father's funeral.

Staring at me he said,
"Where's the casket?"

I volunteered, "There is none.
He wanted to be cremated."

"And you LET HIM?"
His words felt like a punch.

"It was his wish." The blood drained
from my face. He paused, then said,

"I am Aaron, he was my father."
"I am Michael, he was my father, too."

With a half-smile he said, "Then we
are brothers. Why do you look so pale?"

"Forgive my shock.
I didn't know I had a brother."

He retorted, "My mother told me
not to come. She was his secret."

"Wait. Who is your mother?
Where is your mother?"

"Ruth. She lives in Israel. Your father,
our father, was there for a summer

years ago. They loved each other.
He left not knowing about me. I don't

want anything from you."
I was silent, didn't know what to say.

Then he said, "Please,
may I have half his ashes?"

Readers can roost inside a poem.

≈YP≈

LOST PIRATE GOLD

I wanted to be a pirate
since the 4th grade production of *Peter Pan*.
All my closest friends played lost boys, but
I was a pirate, one of a lawless, loathsome crew.
The boy who played Captain Hook
was the coolest kid in the entire school.
He danced around swinging his hook.
Why couldn't I be him?

I came home and told my parents I wanted
to be a pirate. They agreed on the condition
I didn't run away from home. I said okay and
my mother redid my room with pirate wallpaper.
When my parents made me take dance lessons,
I went, as long as I also learned how to do a
sailor's jig. In high school when my friends
and I used fake ID's to go to bars two towns
over, they'd order beers. I only drank rum.

In college, fraternity boys were too tame.
I spent my time in bars down by the docks
listening to sailors tell yarns of exotic places.
I graduated with honors as my parent wished
and gave them my diploma. I framed it for them.
My mother told me, "Do some good with
your life." My father made me a deal.
Go to law school, pass the bar,
and he'd buy me any car I wanted.

I went. I passed. I bought a bright yellow
Mustang with a black stripe down its length. I
named it "Polly." I joined a crew of lawyers
that specialized in bankruptcy. It was a natural
fit for me. We could take a company down, cut
its contractual obligations to shreds and turn
a substantial profit before sailing on to the next
target. We were so good, I made more money
than any thirty-year-old knew what to do with.

I had a gorgeous, golden-haired girlfriend.
We cruised to distant islands and drank daiquiris
in dark bars. She loved the jewels I gave her.
That relationship didn't last, but each Christmas
I went home, showered my parents with gifts,
treasures from around the world.
I think they liked them.
They didn't say much.

I'd spend a lot of my visit in my old room
staring at the wallpaper, picking out
my favorite pirates like I use to,
recalling the 4th grade play,
being a pirate.
Now I wonder,
when did I become
a lost boy?

WITHOUT MERCY

The sin squad knocked on my door.
I quaked at the sight of them.
"We want you to join us,
for you are without sin."

I held my tongue.
They first assigned me
to simple sins, a lover's lie,
a politician's promise.

Each time I spoke to a sinner,
it multiplied my public purity.
My righteous ego grew
taller than a Cedar in Lebanon.

I applied myself assiduously,
and was rewarded with greater sins,
a swindler of widows,
a kidnapper of orphans.

I punished them all, even the penitent.
I was cynical and without mercy.
Then one day
the sin squad knocked on my door.

I HOWL

I howl
because
that's all I
can do.

I howl
because
I'm flawed and
can't accept it.

I howl
because
I hurt and
cause hurt.

I howl
because
I see blood
that's not mine.

I howl
because
there are wounds
that won't heal.

I howl.

A poem
at its best
is a projectile.

MY FATHER'S CHAIR

I remember my father's chair -
big and red and cold
to me in my pajamas,
but its leather - soft
like my mother's skin.
I'd climb up and shuffle back
till I was nestled into it,
but only when he was away.
I felt safe in its wide arms.
Sometimes I'd fall asleep
and dream that he was
sitting in his chair
with me on his lap,
surrounded by his arms.
I love this chair. It's been
in my living room now
for twenty-five years.

UNCLE MILTY AND ME

Uncle Milty,
a compact man,
not really my uncle,
more a close friend of my parents,
drove a New York City cab.
He had no kids and
a wife who didn't smile.
When they visited,
my mother's pot roast,
served with little white potatoes
and yellow corn,
prepared only for special guests,
made Uncle Milty smile.
After dinner
he waved me closer and
I could smell the cigars in his shirt pocket.
I believed him when he cautioned me,
Catfish are really baby sharks.
He had no reason to lie.
Then, he gave me a quarter,
told me to buy some candy.
I think he wanted one of us
to be happy.

RAW AND UNCOOKED
(SEVENTIES SELF-HELP)

A person's raw, uncooked portion
sits in an oven without distortion
until the heat of its own making
is hot enough to finish the baking.

NUTS AND DEATH

Nuts –
I said nuts.
Salty, crunchy.
Home, to me, is
where the nut jar lives.
Cocktails at 4 with my wife,
we talk about our day over
drinks and dry roasted nuts.
When I was a kid, my father kept
a bag of nuts from the 5 & 10 in his
coat pocket. I recognized back then
the advantage of having one's own nuts.
Dad knew how to live. When I was 24, I was
the last one to see him alive. He died quietly,
alone. I miss him. I miss the answers he never
gave me to questions I never thought to ask. We
were two peanuts inhabiting the same hard shell,
unable to get through the divide that separated us.

HOW I MET MY WIFE

As an 18-year-old lifeguard
on top of the world,
I sat alone waiting to save others,
but she shyly approached, smiled,
and saved me. It was 1968.
Her smooth, tanned skin
played hide-and-seek
with her pale bikini.
From my perch I stared far too long.
She asked me if I liked the Beatles.
Trying to be cool I asked her why.
She replied, "I could never marry anyone
who didn't like the Beatles."
I jumped off my lifeguard's chair,
looked into her innocent eyes, and
told her, "Ringo's my favorite."

GROW OLD WITH ME

Will you grow
old with me?
Live quietly
by the sea?
Raise flowers
and sip tea,
while I write
and rewrite
my poetry?

When the sun's
above the horizon
a crack,
we'll lie
a bit longer
belly to back,
without a care
for the things
we lack,
wealthy
in our wordless
love pact.

My mind
is wider than the sky.

after Emily Dickinson

≈YP≈

MORNING LIGHT - MY LIFE

I do not add light to the arriving morning,
or fill the cool air with sweet bird sounds,
or pull the tides to one side like the moon,
I simply groan quietly, not to wake my wife,

and shimmy out of my side of the bed and
head for the toilet and then the kitchen,
where the Cuisinart dutifully did its Maxwell
House task without fuss, or complaint.

My life is filled with small pleasures like my
morning coffee, and persistent pains like my
back barking about its age. I am contently caught
in the limitations and rituals of my life.

MY FUNERAL POEM

If I could live just a little longer,
I'd join the others to mourn
my death. I'd shake their hands
and smile at the sweet things
they're saying about me, cry
over my daughters' recollections,
hug my wife one more time,
thank her for her great generosity.
I would not send myself flowers,
a waste of money, dead in days.
I'd laugh at the Rabbi's attempt
to make my death acceptable.
I'd poke him with my elbow and
tell him don't discount death.
I wasn't done, still had poems to write.

SAVED IN THE CLOUD

Affordable Plans
Yes, we have a plan
for every pocketbook,
for every discriminating taste.

All credit cards accepted.
We know and understand
your dilemma: what to do
with your loved one.

Our online burial is certain
to meet your needs. There is
no mess, no smell, no cleanup.
No waiting or inconvenience.

Our form takes less than
1.5 minutes to complete.
A unique IP will be assigned
to your cherished one
for future reference.

Our two months of experience
tells us you will be satisfied.
In addition, we provide you
a money-back, unconditional
guarantee.

THE PROFESSOR, THE ASSISTANT
AND BABY MAKE THREE

I'm pregnant.
Professor, you're not pregnant.
I think my assistant is.
How do you know?
She's acting funny.
Have you asked her?
No, I'm embarrassed.
Why?
I told her I didn't need protection at my age.
What were you doing in Biology class, writing poetry?
I was writing poetry in the library when we met.
She liked what she saw.
You or the poetry?
We went out for coffee and she invited me
to her place.

So, you had to go?
I did.
At your age, shouldn't you be more careful?
I don't want to be.
You're 65.   She's 30 something.
What are you going to do?
I'm going to ask her.
Ask her if she's pregnant?
No, if she'll marry me.
Think she'll say yes?
I'll ask her in a poem.
One that doesn't rhyme.

MADAM P

Poetry,
my mistress and muse,
demanding and flirtatious,
on occasion, adulterous as April.
Box cutter sharp –
with just the cock of her head
she can open me up,
expose my gut and sinew.
No frailty is safe with her,
no secret too sacred to expose.
She revels in the rhythm of my words.
Dances to the sound of their samba.
The click of her approaching steps
makes me anxious and then,
when I least expect her to,
she pleases me.

GREEN CHEESE

She really believed
the moon was made
of the moldy green cheese
the blogger portrayed.

She read it on his site,
one she trusted the most;
told her neighbor about it
over tea, jam and toast.

The neighbor said
she'd read the fact before,
a headline in the paper
she saw at the store.

Her husband told her
"No, I saw it on cable.
The moon's the final resting place
of Marilyn and Gable."

"How can that be true?
I heard from those who know
Marilyn's still alive
living free in Monaco."

The moon may be made
of moldy green cheese,
but Marilyn and Gable,
that's only a tease.

GRASSHOPPERS AND ANTS

Grasshoppers and ants
wearing shirts and pants,
both blessings and rants,
some cans and some can'ts.

Her name was Megs,
he liked her long legs.
After finishing two kegs,
they married and laid eggs.

Blessings and rants,
some cans and some can'ts,
grasshoppers and ants
wearing shirts and pants.

She knew he was a winner,
but she was a sinner.
He was so much thinner,
she ate him for dinner,

It's fate and it's chance,
both blessings and rants,
grasshoppers and ants,
some cans and some can'ts.

STILL ROAMING

When I was a child
I was sure, if I let my arm
hang over the edge of my bed,
alligators crawling on the floor,
would bite my hand.

Turning on the lights
never proved this to be true,
but I knew they hid
under my bed until
the room was dark.

Even now I won't hang my arm
over the edge of my bed.
I keep it close to my chest,
or under my pillow
to support my head.

For I know, my childhood
alligators still roam the floor,
and should I feel adult enough
to hang my hand, they would
feast on my fingers once more.

Some childhood certainties
never grow up.

SANDWICH SHOP ANGEL

In line, in front of Patty, a goliath stands
blocking her view of *Today's Specials*.

His sleeveless, leather jacket reveals tattooed,
barbell arms, beneath a honeydew head.

He orders a large coffee and sandwich
with extra meat.

The young girl behind the counter asks his name
to put on the order. "Hammer," he replies.

Turning around, he studies Patty. "Ma'am, do
you have the time?" She holds up her left wrist.

No watch. He nods. "Hammer, your food is
ready." He turns back toward the counter,

pays, heads for the door. A few heartbeats later,
Patty hears a motorcycle rev. She turns to look,

but stops. He might be watching. A hand
touches her shoulder. She jumps. "Patty, it's Lisa.

You look pale. Did you see that Hell's Angel?
He smiled at me and held the door.

I wasn't sure if I should thank him,
or run."

Poems don't explain.

≈YP≈

MY AFTERNOON WITH CICERO

I can feel Cicero's breath
on my ear as he whispers,
"Don't be afraid of death. I'm not.

Either the soul is eternal
or it dies with the body.
I'll know soon enough.

Anyway, nature has a plan for me
and I'm closer to its end
than the beginning.

I definitely wouldn't want
to start over again.

When you are young, you have
passion and physical strength.
Be glad. Take advantage.

Let your youthful desires run,
so you don't miss them
in old age when they're gone.

I have no need
for sword or fast horse.
My battles are bloodless.

Now, I have more time
for other things, like repose
in the soft light of afternoon.

There's time for me to share council
with no need for profit. My words
are few, but they are arrows.

Now I plant trees and grow grapes.
Their shade and wine will be
a joy for my great grandchildren.

The old have arrived where
the young can only hope to go."

Cicero smiled at me,
then closed his eyes
for his afternoon nap.

SEVEN DECADES DOWN,
THREE TO GO

I wear a beret of thin grey hair.
My body has scratches and dents
like an abandoned '57 Dodge.
I hear only half of what is said to me;
even less, if you ask my wife.

I'm up early, tired by noon,
in bed before ten.
I sleep with dreams I don't understand.
They bubble up, from
an unsettled past.

I'm not done driving that Dodge,
still wishing it were a convertible
giving me more precious time,
time in the sun, more
time in the sun.

REPAIR BY THE SHORE

The sign over his garage door proclaims,
BEACH CHAIRS CAREFULLY REPAIRED.
Each morning he sits in front of his business
on a sturdy one and waits for customers.

A grey neighbor lady yearning for company
brings him an old chair in terrible shape, says,
"You can have it for parts, no charge.
Tell me, what are you doing for dinner?"

Two small boys living with their grandmother
bring him a chair they found at the curb. He
offers them a quarter, but they want more.
He settles and gives them each fifty cents.

It's been six years since his wife,
the women he thought he could never win,
had a heart attack, lingered and died.
After a year of tears, he had no more.

He decided to start a business. So, he put up
his sign and now sits and waits for people
to come to him who need repair.
Mostly, he collects parts and a few smiles,

as he sits in front of his open garage door.

UNSCRUBBED ONE

The old sailor
with untrimmed beard
and frayed flannel shirt, who still
watches for the perfect sunset
and a calm sea,
gives me a look
for asking too many questions,
embarrasses a young girl
by giving her a smile,
and falls asleep,
just when the minister
gets to the meat
of his sermon.

UNSCRUBBED TWO

The old poet
with untrimmed beard
and frayed turtleneck, who still
pans for new word nuggets
revealing his secrets,
gives me a look
for listening to his conversation,
embarrasses a young girl
by giving her a compliment,
and falls asleep,
just when the minister
gets to the part
about sin.

A good poem
begs for a second reading.

ABOUT THE AUTHOR AND
THE ARTIST

Richard Morgan lives with his wife, artist Pat Morgan in the mountains of western North Carolina. They have published seven books of his words and Pat's watercolors.

As a teacher for over forty years, Richard encourages his readers and listeners to enjoy poetry (especially when they think they won't) and urges them to express their feelings in their own poetic words. Previously, while living on Long Beach Island in New Jersey, he founded The Poets Studio for local writers. Poets shared their works and received constructive feedback, so essential for improvement.

Pat Morgan is a signature member of the North East Watercolor Society, the New Jersey Water Color Society, Audubon Artists, Inc. and a former elected member of the Salmagundi Club in NYC. She has received local and regional awards in NY and NJ.

Pat has been teaching watercolor for 15 years and when not in her gardens, enjoys sharing her love of painting with her students.

Made in the USA
Monee, IL
05 July 2020